Long Lost Sisters

By Sarah Young

Long Lost Sisters
Published by Createspace Independent Publishing Platform, 2016.

ISBN-13: 978-1537604800.
ISBN-10: 1537604805.

Text © Sarah Young.

The rights of Sarah Young to be identified as the Author of this Work have been asserted by her in accordance with the Copyright, Designs and Patents Act, 1988.

All rights reserved. This book is sold under the condition that no part of it may be reproduced, copied, stored in a retrieval system or transmitted in any form or by any means, electronic, mechanical, photocopying, recording or otherwise without prior permission in writing of the author Sarah Young.

Cover photographs: Clifford Young.

Editing, book design: Jim Bruce (www.ebooklover.co.uk).

Contents

Preface .... page 5
Chapter 1: My wonderful childhood ....…...... page 6
Chapter 2: Secret discovery .... page 11
Chapter 3: The search begins .... page 13
Chapter 4: Sister discovered .... page 15
Chapter 5: Reunion Down Under .... page 21
Our family photo album .... page 29
Chapter 6: Back to our roots .... page 36
Chapter 7: Second trip to Oz ....…............... page 41
Chapter 8: The full Monty .... page 44
Chapter 9: Lesley's story .... page 50
Chapter 10: Julia's story ....…... page 63
Acknowledgements .... page 67

Dedication

I dedicate this book to our families, and to all those looking for somebody. Never give up – that someone is somewhere

My Sisters

*What you mean to me,
Is more than I can express.
You see, I had no sisters when I was little,
To call when I was in distress.*

*God had a plan,
Throughout all the years,
He was making us for each other,
To share life's smiles and tears.*

*I never could have imagined,
What sisters' love was about,
Until I met each of you,
And then I really found out.*

*A sister's love is unconditional,
It's a love which has no end,
A sister's love wants the best for each other,
It's a love that will always defend.*

*Because I did not have,
A sister in the past,
It's made me much more thankful,
For the sisters I have at last.*

Preface

WHEN I was a child, I found some hidden family papers that showed I had been adopted – but I never raised the issue with my adoptive parents. Then, in my mid-60s, I was stunned to uncover the full family secret – I had been adopted as an eight-month-old baby.

I then set about trying to find out who my birth parents were, and in the process I was amazed to discover that I had siblings – three sisters I never knew existed, with two of them now living on the other side of the world.

I also found out that we are all related to the Second World War hero, Field Marshall Bernard 'Monty' Montgomery, our great uncle.

This is the remarkable story of my voyage of discovery and the glorious reunion of me and my new-found siblings.

Chapter 1
My wonderful childhood

I WAS adopted when I was eight months old, in October 1945. I was very fortunate to have had a wonderful upbringing and my adoptive parents, Scylla and Mac, loved me very much, which I am very grateful for. I was quite strictly brought up, particularly by my mother, but I realise now that this was because she had such high ideals herself, and she wanted me to be the same. But I was a rebellious child, and we had a few quite intensive arguments, particularly as a teenager! I was their only child; we lived in a small village called Burton, near Christchurch, which in those days was in Hampshire, but with boundary changes in the sixties became Dorset.

My father was always the one I could wrap round my little finger! He and I got on so well. He was very clever in so many ways. He worked at the Ministry of Defence in London and travelled abroad a lot, mostly to America. He was a nuclear physicist, and was instrumental in protecting Britain and other countries from nuclear attack, and his legacy lives on to this day. He was honoured in this country and invested by The Queen with the Knights Companion of the Order of the Bath, which is presented for service of the highest calibre. He was also honoured by the Americans, who presented him with the Defence Medal, a very rare honour.

My father could turn his hand to anything – plumbing, building work, car maintenance, carpentry. He loved Jaguar cars and was always doing something to them, even putting in new engines! One of my fondest memories is as a small child helping him in his workshop (he always found something I could do, usually involving a broom to brush up the shavings!) He loved making things from wood, and as I write this I am sitting at his oak dining room table that he made, which I have great pleasure in using every day. Although so clever, he was always very down-to-earth and had a great sense of humour. He loved making up limericks, and we had great fun doing this on long car journeys!

When I was five years old, my father was posted to Germany. I can remember everything being packed up in tea chests, some to take with us and some to go into storage. The cottage in Burton, where we lived, was let for four years, unfortunately to some not very good tenants, and it was not looked after very well.

Our belongings were flown to Dusseldorf, and we followed in the car, a 1935 Jaguar! The house we were assigned to by the army was in Hahn, a small town near Dusseldorf. I remember the house quite clearly – it was attractive and had a lovely cherry orchard in the garden. The cherries were a cooking variety, and I would keep on trying to eat them hoping they would get sweeter! And of course I ended up with tummy ache!

I was given an old tricycle, which I loved and rode it round and round the garden, as fast as I could. I can remember being given two white rabbits by the wife of General Foote, who was Daddy's boss. And I kept white mice in my bedroom! So my love of animals started at a very young age. We were also given a Dachshund at about this time, called Hannah, who lived until she was 17.

We moved again after a short time to Herford, a bigger town nearby. This time the house we were given was not pleasant at all. It was very big and had an unpleasant atmosphere. My mother always said she was convinced that something evil had taken place there (as the houses that the army allocated belonged to the Nazis originally, this probably could have been the case).

My father was a Lieutenant-Colonel in the army and as an officer was entitled to have a maid to help my mother in the house. Our first maid was called Maria. One day my mother went out and left Maria in charge of me. This was a mistake, because as soon as my mother left, Maria decided to go to the local beer garden, and took me with her! I remember a search party had to be put into action and the ensuing fuss that was made when my mother returned to find her daughter missing! Maria eventually returned with me to a very angry reception! Somehow she was given another chance and stayed. But it wasn't long before her final misdemeanour happened. She was out one evening and was supposed to be back by a certain time, and was late. My father heard a noise in the coal cellar and went down to investigate. There he discovered Maria, sliding down the coal shoot, covered in coal dust and drunk! This was the final straw and she was given her marching orders after this. I wonder what happened to her in the end.

We had two part-time maids after this; both lived out and came in every day. One day my mother said she would like chicken for lunch. A little later, my mother heard strange noises coming from the kitchen. There she discovered the maid about to wring the neck of a rather scrawny-looking chicken! Needless to say chicken was off the menu for lunch that day!

I am recollecting these memories of my early childhood in Germany, while staying in Exeter with Ronnie and Dorothy Curd. I am helping their daughter Sue look after them while their son and daughter-in-law have a holiday. Ronnie and Dorothy met my parents in Germany. Ronnie was a captain and met my father on an army exercise. Ronnie is now 102 and Dorothy is 96 and they have been married for 72 years! They are a truly remarkable couple and I am very fond of them. Sue, their son Richard and I used to spend lots of time together as children, so they are all very special to me. It seems so applicable that I should be recalling these memories while staying with them, and hearing some of their memories too!

We had some good times in Germany. I particularly remember a holiday we had in Bavaria. We stayed in an old farmhouse. I have such vivid memories; it must have made quite an impression on me. The beautiful scenery, the lakes and mountains, and the high narrow roads with frightening hairpin bends!

I went to school in the army barracks in Herford. It was just like the army really! The headmistress was horrible – very, very strict! She had red hair and I was terrified of her, I think we all were! We were not allowed to talk in the corridors, and I was caught talking to a little boy. We were both given several whacks across our hands with a stick. It really hurt, the little boy cried, but I can remember trying so hard not too!

Just after I started school, Goldie came into our lives. He was the most beautiful dog, part German shepherd and part Afghan hound. He had been trained as an army police guard dog but was found to be too gentle for that! So he had been passed round to different families as a pet, but as each new owner was posted somewhere else, so poor Goldie was passed on again. We were about the third or fourth family that he came to. I adored him and he loved me. He would wait for me at the garden gate when it was time for me to come home from school, and he would follow me everywhere. At Christmas time, it was the German tradition that the front door should be kept unlocked and carol singers would just come in and start singing. Goldie was not happy with this arrangement and barked and growled at them! The poor carol singers scattered all over the house! We managed to gather them all up again and Goldie was introduced to them properly, and they realised that his bark was far worse then his bite! Whenever I hear Silent Night sung in German it reminds me of this story.

I was lucky enough to have riding lessons on Saturday mornings, which I loved. We were taught by a Polish ex-cavalry officer. He was very strict, and I can still remember him teaching us the trot, going round and round him, and shouting "Up! Down! Up! Down!" I have always felt very fortunate that I was taught to ride by an ex-cavalry officer!

In 1954, after four years, we came back to England. We brought Goldie and Hannah the Dachshund home with us, and they both lived long and happy lives. I look back at the time we spent in Germany with great fondness, except for the start I had at school!

My mother was also very busy and involved with a number of good causes. She always seemed to be going to committee meetings! She was very involved with what was then called Displaced Persons, which was the name given to refugees from Europe after the war. There was a large house in Barton-on-Sea, in Hampshire, near Christchurch, where we lived, which was run by volunteers as a refuge. My mother took me with her many times to help with the activities. I can remember playing snap a lot, and Scrabble to help the refugees with their English, although my spelling was not brilliant, so looking back I'm not sure if I was much help! They were mostly from Poland and Czechoslovakia.

My mother was also involved with the Guide Dogs for the Blind, and helped run the local WRVS (Women's Royal Voluntary Service) and organised the Meals on Wheels service. So she was always busy!

Chapter 2
Secret discovery

WHEN I was about nine or ten years old, I became very curious about things. For a long time I had a feeling that I didn't quite fit in. I can't quite describe my feelings just that something was missing.

One day I found myself alone in the house. I decided to do some investigation to see what I could discover. I knew that at the top of my parents' wardrobe there were several file boxes and briefcases. When I look back at it now, I wonder how I had the nerve! My mother could have come back at any time! I managed to lift the boxes and briefcases down, and opened one of the boxes. Inside were a lot of papers. They looked very official – they must have been my adoption papers. On the first document was my birth name, Penelope Valentine Jones. I can remember feeling quite sick from the shock of seeing this. I shall never forget that day! My name was seared into my brain for years afterwards. I never felt strong enough to admit to my parents about what I had discovered, so I kept it secret for many, many years.

When I look back at my childhood, I must have had quite a lot of freedom. I spent a lot of time at the dairy farm next door to our cottage. I loved helping with the milking and having rides on the cart at hay-making time. In the field there was an old shire horse that I called Dobbin. I loved horses and still do, and he fulfilled my need to be near horses. One day, in a dark and cobwebby shed, I found his old harnesses. I decided to try and get his bridle on. By this time he hadn't been used for any farm work for quite a few years, so it must have been a shock for him to have his bridle on again! I can remember having to find something to stand on to reach his head. What freedom I must have had to get up to all this mischief!

That poor horse — what I put him through. I even tried to get him to jump! He was so patient with me. I am ashamed now to think about how at school, I always tried to make friends with girls who had horses or ponies. It seemed to work pretty well, and I spent many weekends and school holidays staying with them. There were lots of horse shows going on most weekends, so they were always practising their jumping or showing. In the winter there was hunting, which I loved, and if no horse was available, I would follow the hounds on my bike!

Chapter 3
The search begins

MY father died very suddenly in November 1993, aged 78. It was such a shock to us all. My mother was devastated, of course, and missed him dreadfully. I experienced for the first time the pain of bereavement. It was a difficult time, and I tried to help her as much as possible. The tributes from all over the world that were paid to him was evidence of how highly my father was regarded.

My mother suffered from cancer for many years. She was so brave and never complained. I tried to look after her, and was with her during her final illness.

A few days before she died, aged 81 in March 1999, she asked me to fetch her glasses from a drawer. When I opened the drawer, in the front was a piece of paper. Written on it was 'Important Dates in My Life'. The first event was Penelope Valentine born 14.2.45, came to me October 1945. I am sure my mother sent me to that drawer so I would see it. Unfortunately, she was not able to communicate at all after this, and within a few hours her brave fight with cancer was over.

After my mother died I felt I would like to try and find out more information about myself. The law had changed so that adopted people were at last able to find out more about themselves.

I had to apply to Social Services to get this information. After some delay I was invited to attend an interview with a social worker and to receive some counselling. I was a bit put of by this, but the intention was to make sure that I was prepared for any problems. I attended the interview, and the social worker explained that because my adoption was conducted privately, there was very little information on my file. However she did have my full birth certificate, which was a big breakthrough, as it had my birth parents' full names!

My mother was Ethel Wilhemina Delatte, her father was Dutch, and she was born in Lambeth, London, in 1911. My father was James Hamilton Jones, born in Birmingham in 1894. I left the Social Services office in a bit of a flutter.

Armed with this information I tried to find out some more. I decided to go to the Family Records Office in London to do some research. It was an amazing place. From floor to ceiling, on thick shelves there were huge ledgers, they had a very old appearance with beautiful copperplate writing.

I was a bit daunted by what I was trying to do. The staff looked really busy, and everyone else seemed to know what they were doing! I hadn't got a clue where to start. I soon realised that I would not be able to find out anything on the Dutch side, as the records were only for British citizens. So I tried to find out more about my father's side. But I was not successful. I did find details about my adoption, but nothing I didn't already know. So you might think it was a waste of time! But I am very glad I did go, because shortly after my visit, the Family Records Office was closed to the public and all the records were digitalised. I wonder where those old ledgers are now?

Chapter 4
Sisters discovered

AT this time I began to feel rather daunted by what I was trying to do, and I wondered if I was ever going to make any progress. When I had these doubts, something would spur me on again.

I now had a breakthrough. My daughter-in-law's best friend, who lives in Scotland, is very keen on family history. She heard about what I was trying to do and did lots of research for me. She did such a lot to help me, and I am very grateful to her. She traced records for my grandparents and great grandparents. She also told me about Bournemouth Library and its family records department. The Bournemouth area is where my parents were married, lived, and where I was born.

My great friend Phyll lives in Bournemouth, so I decided to visit her and go to the library. Nancy thought it would be a good idea if I contacted the library beforehand to ask them to do some research before I got there.

When Phyll and I arrived, we were met by one of the researchers. She told me straight away that she had some very exciting news for me – the discovery that I had two sisters, Julia and Sarah! Julia was born in 1934 and Sarah in 1953. I was overwhelmed at this incredible news, and was very glad I had Phyll with me!

When I got home, I had to decide where to go from here. My husband Cliff was such a support at this time, listening to me prattle on about my sisters. I had to do some serious thinking about what to do next. There are many considerations to be taken into account in this type of situation. Questions such as: Why was I adopted? What were the circumstances? What about my sisters' lives? What were their circumstances? And of course if contact was thought about, how would this affect their families and their lives? I was having doubts at this stage, and thought perhaps I should leave things alone.

One day our great friends Maureen and Gerry came for supper. I was telling them about my sisters and the difficulties I was having. Gerry had also been adopted and told us his news. He had traced and made contact with his three brothers, through an organisation called Norcap, who help adopted people find their families. This was the breakthrough I needed! Gerry explained that intermediaries are used to make the initial contact, and that a lady called Linda had been his intermediary.

The next day I contacted Norcap. They were very helpful and put me in touch with Linda. I rang her and she was very understanding about the problems I was having. She told me about some of the ways Norcap could use to trace people. They have access to records that cannot be accessed by the public. She agreed to take on my case, and would let me know as soon as she had any news.

About two months later I received a phone call from Linda with some very exciting news. She had managed to trace my eldest sister Julia, living in Australia! I remember the first thought I had was 'Well, that's that then. I'm never going to be able to see her on the other side of the world!' How wrong that turned out to be!

Linda had made the initial contact to Julia by letter, and asked her to ring if she wanted to make contact with me. Julia rang Linda to say she would like to make contact! Linda arranged that I should ring Julia straight away, as it would be early evening in Australia with the time difference.

I was trembling when I made that call! Julia answered the phone, and said "Hello Sarah!" It was the most amazing feeling knowing I was talking to my sister! She sounded so lovely and we talked and talked, we seemed to talk so easily! There was so much information to take in!

Julia told me that there were four sisters – not three! Sarah was number three and was born in 1953. When Julia and Michael got married in 1955, they emigrated to Australia on the ten pound 'Pom' scheme and left Sarah behind with our parents. I was born in 1945 and had already been adopted. Sarah went out to Australia to live with Julia and Michael when she was nine. She has made a successful life for herself and I appreciate that she wishes to maintain her privacy. One day however we hope to meet up with her.

Now for my surprise sister! Zoe was born in July 1955 she was adopted and given the name Lesley. When Julia told me this, of course I knew I had to try to find her.

I think at this stage it might help if I make it clear the order of our births:

1) Julia Ann Wilhelmina Jones. Born April 1934.
2) Penelope Valentine Jones - adopted (me!). Born February 1945.
3) Sarah Hamilton Jones. Born April 1953.
4) Zoe Elizabeth Jones – adopted. Born July 1955.

Julia explained about the circumstances that led up to our adoptions. Our parents, Ethel Wilhelmina De Laat and James Hamilton Jones got married in February 1933 at Bournemouth Register Office. James was an architect and they were quite well off, before the Second World War. Life was good and they had a busy social life. In 1939 at the start of the war life changed dramatically; as it did for so many people.

Julia told me that our mother, Ethel, by this time became a heavy drinker and was an alcoholic. Very sadly this led to our adoptions. What role our father played in all this is not very clear, so I don't really know how he was affected.

This first phone call to Julia lasted two hours! I promised Julia that I would contact Norcap and try to find Zoe, our fourth sister.

I rang Linda to tell her how well my contact with Julia had gone and could she find another one of us! She said she would try, and I told her all we knew was her original birth name. It must have been quite difficult to find her and I was expecting a long wait for any news.

However, two weeks later, Linda rang to say she had found Zoe! The same arrangements were put in place as for the first contact with Julia, and I was to ring Lesley, as this was her name now after her adoption, at her home in Cirencester, Gloucestershire.

As soon as Lesley answered the phone it was wonderful! She was so excited and pleased. We talked and talked, just like with Julia. It was truly amazing for this to be happening again. Lesley is married to Mark and they have two daughters, Gemma and Cheryl. They have partners, Tom and Adam. Gemma and Tom have two little girls, Florence and Edith. Cheryl and Adam have a little boy, Mason, and a little girl, Cassidy.

At this point I must mention Julia's large family in Australia. She and Michael had six children – five girls and one boy. So this meant that suddenly I was an auntie, great aunt, sister, and sister-in-law! And of course Cliff was an uncle, great uncle, and brother-in law!

A few weeks later we arranged to meet up at Windsor, a halfway point between Cirencester and Faversham, where I live. We planned to meet up at a hotel opposite Windsor Castle at noon.

On the journey there, I felt very nervous and apprehensive. Cliff was very reassuring, saying things like "Oh well, if we don't like them, we don't need to take it any further!" We eventually arrived and parked the car, and began walking towards the castle. There were lots of people about, and we wondered how we would find them.

Suddenly, out of the crowd I saw a man running towards us saying: "You must be Sarah, and you must be Cliff!" I remember saying to him: "But how do you know?" Mark laughed and said: "Because you look so like your sister!" We found Lesley and it was an incredible feeling. We hugged and it seemed so right and my nerves vanished!

We went into the hotel and had a coffee. There was so much to talk about, they were such lovely people, and we all got on so well from the very first meeting. What a relief! We decided to go for a meal and found an Italian restaurant nearby. The hours flew by, and all too soon the time came to say goodbye. We all knew it wouldn't be too long before we would meet again.

In the car on the way home I was on a cloud. That first meeting had gone so well, and we hoped they had liked us as much as we liked them.

For the next few weeks, I could not think or talk about anything else. John and Robert, our sons, and Robert's wife Bea, who had all been so supportive to me during this time, were thrilled that our first meeting had gone so well.

Cliff's mother, aged 104, has always shown a great interest in this story. Although understandable at her age, her memory is not good, but she has always remembered about my sisters, and wants to know what's happening.

Our friends have also been very supportive, and they all wanted to meet Mark and Lesley. So we decided to have a get-together with everyone so they could meet them. It was summer so we planned a barbecue. It was a very special day, and everyone seemed to enjoy themselves. It was remarked upon several times by our friends how alike Lesley and I are.

One weekend we went to stay with them in Cirencester to meet their family and friends. This was very special too. I have a very clear recollection of sitting in their garden, watching everyone, and it suddenly dawning on me that the people here were my flesh and blood! My family!

Chapter 5
Reunion Down Under

A FEW months later Cliff, myself, Lesley and Mark began discussing the possibility of going to Australia to see Julia. This idea soon grew and we started making plans. We used a travel company called Freedom Australia to help us with the arrangements. Christine was our rep and she did a fantastic job putting it all together for us.

Our itinerary was as follows:
- Fly to Singapore for two days.
- Singapore-Sydney.
- Sydney- Nowra to stay with Julia.
- Nowra-Sydney to catch the Indian Pacific train to Adelaide for three days.
- Adelaide-Melbourne for three days.
- Melbourne-Sydney.
- Sydney-Cairns.
- Cairns-Brisbane.
- Brisbane-Hong Kong for three days.
- Hong Kong-London.

A trip of a lifetime!

The plans were made, the bags packed, and we were all ready for our trip (and the piggy banks broken into!) We all met up at Terminal 3 Heathrow. The plane was the new Airbus 380. I looked out of a window and saw it parked up, and I could not believe the size of it, and how it would ever be able to take off! I had a few problems with flying, but somehow because I so wanted to see Julia, I managed to get through it.

The flight took eleven hours to Singapore. I was quite pleased with how I managed to cope with the flight. Poor Cliff's arm at take-off and landing! I gripped it so tightly, I was surprised it wasn't bruised!

We were very impressed by Changai terminal. Amazing architecture, I never thought an airport terminal could be so beautiful. Everywhere was so clean and calm. We found our taxi waiting, and went to our hotel. The road from the airport was so beautiful, with flowers growing everywhere. The hotel was very impressive and the rooms were excellent. After we had sorted ourselves out a bit, we went out to explore. I love exploring new places! Singapore is a very serene, calm, and clean city and we all loved it.

The next day we took the hotel shuttle bus and went to the Raffles Hotel. This was the place in the 1920s and 1930s where people like Graham Greene, Noel Coward and royalty would stay. During the war of course it got badly damaged by the Japanese, and was allowed to become derelict after the war. In the 1980s, a group of expats formed a group to try to save it. It is now restored to its former glory. It is really beautiful, and so good to see that it has been saved. There was a very good museum, with lots of photographs of the people who stayed there – Ernest Hemingway, Rudyard Kipling and Sir Winston Churchill, who stayed many times and really loved it. We sat on the terrace and had a Gin Sling, the cocktail that was invented there. Very decadent!

Afterward we went to the war memorial. So many were killed by the Japanese; 50,000 Chinese just disappeared. It was a very impressive memorial and a lovely garden. We then walked to St Andrew's Church, the British Garrison church, all white inside and out. Lots of memorials to British soldiers.

The next day we flew to Sydney. We landed at 6am and went straight to our apartment in Pitt Street, in the city centre. The apartment was 38 floors up and very luxurious. Freedom Australia, our travel company, did a really good job for us. We dropped the bags off and went off to explore. No time to waste! As we went down Pitt Street, the main street in Sydney, I suddenly caught sight of a small section of the Harbour Bridge, in between some skyscrapers. Then we saw the harbour. It really is a fantastic sight. The whole view, the bridge and the Sydney Opera House, is a wonderful sight, and to think that the Opera House nearly didn't get built, because of the controversy at the beginning of its conception.

We then returned to the apartment and tried again to ring Julia. We had tried earlier, but couldn't get through. This attempt was successful, and Julia was so happy to hear from us. We made the arrangements for meeting her at Nowra, which is on the south coast of Australia in New South Wales, about 100 miles south of Sydney. We had worked out there was a train from Sydney Central, changing at Kiama and arriving at Nowra at 12.15.

The next morning we made our way to the station, Mark in the lead, and all of us running to keep up! Bless him, he was so concerned, as we all were, not to miss the train! We managed to catch it and were on our way,

It is about 100 miles from Sydney to Nowra, and it would take about two-and-a-half hours. The trains in Australia are double-deckers, so there is plenty of room. When we arrived at Kiama, there was only four minutes to catch the one for Nowra. This was the part worrying all of us, as there were very few trains to Nowra on this little branch line. But we needn't have worried because the platform was very near. The train was in, and we sat there for forty minutes until it left!

When we arrived at Nowra, the station was very busy, and I wondered how we would be able to spot Julia. I looked towards the entrance, and there she was! She saw us and came towards us. It was such a surreal moment, to be together! We hugged each other, nothing over the top, as this is not our style. We found Julia's car and managed to squeeze the entire luggage in. Then Julia asked would we mind if we stopped at the supermarket to buy some bread! I love this down-to-earth approach to life that we all seem to have! You meet your sisters for the first time and then you go and buy some bread! I loved that! Cliff suggested that we have a coffee (he does love his coffee). This was a good idea, actually, because it gave us a chance to sit down and catch our breath a bit.

We then went to the B&B that Julia had booked for us. We dropped the bags off, and Julia took us to her house nearby. Gillian, Julia's youngest daughter, was there to meet us. She gave us a lovely welcome. A barbecue had been planned for us to meet the family. There are a lot of them. Julia and Michael had six children – one boy, Roger, and five girls, Katherine, Tanya, Sharon, Kerry and Gillian. There are lots and lots of grandchildren and great grandchildren, mostly girls, all tall, blonde and blue eyes!

People began arriving, and I had trouble remembering all their names! I volunteered to do the prawns for the 'barbie' and I had a seemingly never-ending flow of lovely, tall, blonde girls coming along to help me! One would come along, introduce themselves, do a few prawns, tell me a bit about themselves, and then somebody else would take over! And all my nieces!

Kathy, who is Julia's eldest daughter, arrived with her girls, Kayla and Ellie. She lives nearby, and we got to know her very well.

We had such a memorable time meeting everyone, it was such a happy day, and one of the many memories that I treasure.

Unfortunately, the time flew by and people began to leave. However, Kathy was not leaving yet because she and Julia had sorted some photos out for us to see. We had a lovely time looking at photos of our parents, grandparents, and various members of the family. This meant a great deal to Lesley and I to see these photos of our family.

We learnt such a lot that evening. One photo particularly sticks in my mind. It is one of our parents taken before the war. They both look so happy, when life was good. We learnt about our Auntie Kath. She was our father's sister and was a Suffragette! We are very proud of that!

Something else that surprised us was when Julia mentioned Monty! Our ears pricked up and we asked: "Did you say Monty? The Monty?" And Julia replied: "Oh yes, of course, you don't know about him, do you?" Well, no Julia, we don't! Our father's sister was Monty's mother! Which makes war hero Field Marshall Montgomery (Monty) our great uncle! What a family!

We had had such a special day with Julia and our family, and by now it was getting late, so Kathy offered to take us back to the B&B. And so ended a very memorable day.

The next day, Julia picked us up from the B&B. She had planned a trip for us to see whales at Jervis Bay. This bay is on the main migratory route for blue whales and their calves. We had some fantastic sightings of them – what a thrill!

Julia then took us to a nearby beach. It was amazing. The sand was white, and the sea so blue, I couldn't believe what I was seeing. The pictures you see in travel brochures look so unreal, but in fact beaches really can look like that. We just chilled out, walking, talking, paddling. Cliff and Mark did a wonderful job of taking photographs of us three, and I have one in a frame that I look at every day.

Julia then took us back to her house for the evening, and we heard more about when she and Michael started their life in Australia. They went out from England on the £10 emigration scheme in the 1950s. Julia tells the story of how they set off with a tractor and trailer and a few bits of furniture, just like the early pioneers, to a diary farm in the

Kangaroo Valley, which is in the Southern Highlands of New South Wales.

Eventually, they managed to get enough money together to buy some outback land, with a small building on it. Michael (who sounds like he was a very determined character) decided they would try and turn this land into a strawberry farm. Julia had her doubts when she saw the state of the land, but tried to keep them to herself. It must have been incredibly hard work, to turn it into productive and fertile land, but they managed it, and from all accounts it became a successful venture.

They sold the strawberries at local shops and markets, and local people came to the farm. In those days, strawberries were comparatively rare, and they were almost a luxury item, so it was a good time to produce them. The girls were known locally as the Morley Strawberry Girls, because they had to pull their weight and work hard to help on the farm. Later on when I asked Kathy about their childhood, she told me they were expected to help, but also had a lot of freedom. It sounded like an idyllic childhood. They would go off for the day, with their ponies, and not get back until the evening.

When you see the land now it's hard to imagine it as scrubby outback land. It looked so verdant and green when we were there.

Julia also took us to Booderee National Park, about an hour from her home in Nowra. Julia remembers it as it used to be: Aboriginal land mostly, and certainly not called a national park! We walked through a pine forest, lots of areas for barbecues, already set up and built of brick — what a good idea. Suddenly we saw our first kangaroo! I had no idea they were so big! It must have been well over 6ft tall! It had a baby in its pouch; with its legs sticking out, and then somehow managed to fold them back in!

Then I caught sight of the beach. It took my breath away, it was so beautiful. The sea was so blue, the sand so white and it squeaked when you walked on it! We had such a lovely day there. Julia and I had a swim, and I suddenly had a wobbly moment when I thought 'Here I am swimming with my sister!' Lesley wasn't so keen to go in the sea, and neither were the men! I really don't know why, it was lovely! The men once again took some lovely pictures and we were so lucky to have two keen photographers.

Julia had planned such memorable days for us and they are memories we will never forget. This was what we thought at the time would be our last day together, but later events would prove this wrong.

The next day we said our goodbyes. We were sad, but hoped that one day we would see each other again – and indeed we did!

We left Sydney on the magnificent Indian Pacific train to Adelaide. What an adventure this was. We all loved it. Seeing Australia by train really gives an idea of the vastness of this country. From Adelaide we went to Melbourne on the Overlander train, and then flew up to Cairns in far north Queensland. What a trip!

When we got back to Sydney, we had a phone call from Kathy. They had decided to come and see us the next day! Brilliant news!

We met up the next morning with Kathy and her daughters Georgie and Ellie, and Julia. We had such a fun day shopping. The stores in Sydney are fantastic! The girls wanted to shop for shoes, so we went in and out of lots of stores, the girls trying on all these incredibly high heels. How they walked in them, I don't know! They are so tall, like all Julia's girls, but really elegant with it, so they walked in perfect ease in their heels!

We had a lovely meal together in the evening, by the harbour, and then it was time to say our goodbyes. We didn't linger over this, as it was hard to do, but we all hoped to be able to meet again one day.

Our time in Australia was now nearly over. We had such a wonderful time, with memories that we will never forget. I felt so blessed to have had this special time with my sisters. It was so special to get to know them. It was also amazing how Mark, Cliff, Lesley and I, after such a short time of knowing one another, travelled together so well. We all got on! That was a relief.

Our family album

The early years

Sarah's birth father, James Hamilton Jones, and her birth mother Ethel, far right, with a friend at Bournemouth

The earliest pictures of Sarah, born Penelope Valentine Jones, as a baby. Left: probably taken at the mother & baby home (the woman isn't Sarah's mother)

Sarah aged around two (left) and with her adoptive parents, Scylla and Mac, during their time in Germany

Sarah and her dog Goldie in Germany, left, and the thatched cottage where she lived as a child in Burton, near Christchurch. Below: In the MG car with her mum

Sarah's adoptive parents, left, and later in the 1980s, above

Sister Julia – past and present

Above: Julia's wedding to Michael Morley

Above: Julia with Dutch grandfather Jachabus and grandmother Ethel

Right: The first photo Julia sent to Sarah

The first trip to Australia

Lesley and Sarah at Sydney Harbour, with the famous Opera House behind

Above: Lesley, Sarah and Cliff are all smiles on their trip to Sydney

Mark, left, Cliff, Sarah and Lesley at Sydney Harbour, with the city's famous harbour bridge in the background

Georgie, far left, her sister Ellie and their mum Kathy, with Lesley, Julia and Sarah at Sydney Harbour

Kathy with her daughters Ellie, left, and Georgie

The sisters at Hyams beach

Julia, left, just couldn't resist trying on a hat during the shopping trip to Sydney with her two sisters and her family

Julia & Kathy's trip to England in 2012

In Sarah's garden, from left: Kathy, Linda Cherry from Norcap, Cliff, Sarah, Lesley, friend Laura, Julia and Mark

Back row: Cliff, friends Mary and Trevor (he's on the right) and Mark.

Bottom row: Sarah, Julia, Lesley and Kathy

Lesley and Mark's family

Lesley & Mark with Tom (holding Florence), left, Edith (with Gemma), Cheryl (with Mason) and Adam (holding Cassidy)

Sarah and Cliff's family

Sarah and Cliff with their sons Robert, left, and John, right

Chapter 6
Back to our roots

AFTER we arrived back in the UK, I thought a lot about my sisters. I hoped that before too long we would be able to meet up again. I had no idea how or when, so it was a wonderful surprise to get the news that Julia and daughter Kathy had decided to come over to the UK in 2012. This was very exciting, and we began making plans for their visit. They were planning to come in September and stay for three weeks. We knew of a lovely B&B nearby in an old Kentish farmhouse that we thought they would like, so we booked it for them.

Then in May came more exciting news. Kylie, Kathy's daughter, and her friend Kyla sent me an email to say they were planning a trip to Europe and asked if they could stay with us for a few days. Of course the answer was yes! They are lovely girls and we all had such fun. We took them to London and met up with Mark and Lesley, and showed them the sights.

When it was time for them to leave for the rest of their trip, it was sad to see them go, we so enjoyed their stay with us.

Plans were now well advanced for Julia and Kathy's stay with us. It was the first time Julia had been back to the UK since she emigrated, and the first time for Kathy. Julia had spoken of her wish to see Bournemouth and the surrounding area while they were here, because that's where we all originated from, so it would mean a lot to all of us. Mark and

Lesley's great friends Mary and Gary, who live in the area, found us a mobile home and booked it up for us. This was ideal, as it would give us the freedom to come and go as we liked.

Soon the day of their arrival came. I was so excited. We arranged for a taxi to pick them up at Heathrow, and they arrived here at 9am. What joy to have my sister and my niece to stay! We took them to the B&B and Mrs. Scutt, the owner, gave them a lovely welcome (she had of course been told the story!) They were very impressed by the house, and Kathy couldn't believe how old the building was, as parts of it date back to the 1400s.

The next day Mark and Lesley arrived for the weekend, and I had to pinch myself when I thought of both my sisters being here in my house!

The next day we had arranged for some friends to join us for lunch at our favourite old pub. I had asked Linda, our Norcap intermediary, if she could join us, as I felt it would be lovely for her to meet my sisters, and Mark and Kathy. This she was able to do, which I was very pleased about, because without her and Norcap none of this would be happening. She was so pleased to be with us, and to see the results of all her hard work. It was a lovely day.

After this our next was our trip to Bournemouth. We had a good journey and found the caravan site where the mobile home was.

We did such a lot on this trip, and Julia was so pleased to see the area again, and to be able to show Kathy where it all began. We went to Christchurch. This was where our parents met, married and lived before and after the war ended. We found the flat in the High Street, over a charity shop, which bizarrely was called Julia's House – a local children's hospice charity. We found this quite spooky, in a way. The thought suddenly occurred to me that this is where our mother Ethel would have been pregnant with me, Lesley and Sarah. Our mother would have been pregnant with Julia when they lived at Hengistbury Head.

We did find the house where they lived. Our father was an architect and we think he probably designed and had the house built, as it had an individual style about it. This was at the time when our parents had money. Julia even had a nanny!

While we were in Christchurch, we found the pub where Julia met Michael for the first time. We went in and had a coffee, and Julia thought it looked much the same as it did then. I thought about all this from Kathy's point of view, and how she must be feeling, realising that this is where it all began! Her parents meeting here for the first time, and now with all the children, grandchildren and great grandchildren!

Lesley had one of her lightbulb moments, as she does, and had made a list of all the addresses in the Bournemouth area with connections to our family. So the next day, Mark and Cliff did a fantastic job of driving us round, to try to find them, which we did! I saw where the mother and baby home had been — it is now a block of flats — where I was born.

Lesley was born at Barton-on-Sea, but there is no trace of that building. We found where our Dutch grandfather lived just before the war. He worked as a waiter in quite a lot of hotels in Bournemouth, and seemed to move about the country as well.

We then went out to Burton, a village near Christchurch, where I lived as a small child. The village has changed out of all recognition, so I had great difficulty in getting my bearings! We found the pub, the Oak Inn, which I remembered was a few doors down from The Thatch, the cottage where we lived. I stood at the gate of the cottage and the memories started flooding back. It really didn't look that different, just prettied up a bit. We then drove along the lanes, which were just as I remembered them.

When Julia's husband Michael was a young man, he worked on a farm. Suddenly Mark, who was driving in front, screeched to a halt. I got out of the car to see what had happened. Julia had suddenly recognised the name of the farm, on the left hand side, where Michael worked as a young man! It looked as though it hadn't had much done to the upkeep of the buildings, and was probably the same as when he was there. I suddenly realised this was on the route of one of my dog walks, that I used to go on when I was a child. I might even have seen Michael working on the farm.

Later on we found the cottage where Michael used to live. Julia and Kathy were so pleased and thrilled to find these links to Michael. If only he had been with us. Very sadly he died in 1998 after a long illness.

What an eventful day this had been, with so many memories. It really is extraordinary to think how near we all were at the start of our lives, Lesley didn't live there for as long, as when she was adopted she lived near Winchester. My adoptive parents were always going into Christchurch, so it is quite possible I might have seen Julia and our parents. Our sister Sarah stayed with our parents until she was 10 years old, when she went to join Julia and Michael in Australia.

Another memorable day was when we went to Mudeford, near Christchurch. I have some very happy memories of this old fishing village, it was one of our favourite places. Julia has also some happy memories of Mudeford. She told quite alarming stories of when, as a child, she would play with other children, making boats and trying to sail them, which sounded fairly harmless until more details were revealed. They found an old petrol tank from a crashed plane (this was shortly after the war) to make a boat, and tried to float it in what is called The Race, a very dangerous bit of sea. The tide comes in very fast, with strong currents and rip tides. So they were very lucky to survive.

So much happened in those few days, and we packed a lot in. Lesley and Mark's friends, Mary and Gary, arranged for us to have a meal with them, together with Mary's brother and the rest of her family. During the conversation, Julia was talking about the farm where Michael worked, mentioning the name of someone who became best man at their wedding. Mary's brother could not believe it – Julia and Michael's best man turned out to be his first cousin, who is still alive. What a small world! Julia and Kathy were pleased to hear this.

Our time in Dorset was drawing to a close. We had accomplished so much, and we hoped Julia and Kathy would have lots of memories to look back on.

When we arrived back in Kent, Julia and Kathy only had a few days left before they were due to fly back to Australia. We all had such lovely memories of our time together.

The day arrived for their departure. It was hard saying goodbye to them, and we all hoped that we would see one another again in the near future.

Chapter 7
Second trip to Oz

A FEW months later, plans were being made for our second trip to Australia. It was incredible to be lucky enough to be able to go again. Mark contacted Freedom Australia, the travel agent that we used before. We planned to have another train journey on the Indian Pacific, this time from Perth to Sydney, right across from one side of the country to the other, a distance of 2,700 miles.

What a trip that was! It is such a wonderful way to see this amazing country. It really gives an impression of how vast Australia is, the landscape stretching on and on for ever! And the big, big skies!

The train was very comfortable and the food was first-class. We were very well looked after.

When we arrived in Sydney, we stayed in the same apartments as we had on the first trip, but this time we were 45 floors up! When we got there I looked out of the window and realised that there seemed to be something going on down below. Chairs were being arranged, lots of police officers about, and a general feeling of something about to happen. We went down and discovered that we had arrived just in time for the celebrations for the centenary of the Australian Navy. The march past was about to start, with navies from all over the world taking part. The Royal Marines Band were there, and our Royal Navy was represented by HMS Daring.

After we had watched the march past, we went to the harbour. As well as ships from all over the world, there were lots of Tall Ships — what a wonderful sight it all was. Endeavour, the replica of Captain Cook's ship, was there. I suddenly realised that the last time Cliff and I had seen her was in Whitby, Yorkshire, when she was returning to England from Australia. Who would have thought that the next time we would see her would be in Sydney, with my sister and brother-in-law! How incredible was that.

We enjoyed our few days in Sydney very much. It is such a vibrant and welcoming place, we all loved it.

We then took the train down to Nowra to stay with Julia. She met us at the station, and it was such a joy to be together again. We went back to her house, and some of the family arrived. It felt as though we had hardly been away. And we just carried on from where we left off last time we met.

Julia told us that Kathy had managed to rent a house for us all at Hyams Beach, the wonderful beach that Julia took us to on our first visit. We stayed there for five days, and we have such happy memories of this time. The house was like ones you see in magazines, such as Ideal Home! The architecture had been so well executed, and the general layout of the house well thought out and planned — a dream house!

The sea was very near, and that wonderful beach, so I was in paradise! And all thanks to Kathy for arranging it for us. We were all so grateful to her for doing it for us. The house was so big that all our nieces, great nieces and partners could come and go. Some stayed, and I sometimes got confused as to who was still there and who had left! Sometimes someone would appear in the morning whom I was sure had left the night before! It was all such fun and we all loved every minute, especially the evenings. The meals were all planned for us, and the girls all mucked in and cooked them. They would arrive in the evening with bags of shopping, having been to college or work, and set to and made a meal for us! It was so kind of them. Of course we all helped as well and a good time was had by all! One evening I suddenly had a thought that everyone in this house was related to me in some way! I'd come from not knowing who I was to this!

The day arrived for us to return to Julia's house for the remainder of our stay. The next day she had planned to take us to the Kangaroo Valley, where she and Michael first settled when they came to Australia on the ten pound emigration scheme in the 1950s. In those days there were a lot of farms, much smaller then there are now.

We saw a herd of cows crossing the road in front of us, going to be milked, mostly Friesians with a few Guernseys and Jersey cows, to increase the cream in the milk. It was a very large herd – there must have been several hundred!

Julia showed us where the house stood where she and Michael once lived with their children. Sadly all that is left now is the chimney stack sticking out of the ground. We took some photos, and Julia told us what hard work it had been to save up enough money to buy some land of their own.

Julia drove us around a lot, in her old Ute, as the Aussies call their utility vehicles, which most people seem to drive. Her Ute was seventeen years old and still going strong!

One day she took us to see her daughter Kerry, our niece. Everyone that we met remarked how like Kerry I am! As soon as we walked into her house, I could see what they meant! It was just like my house. She collects things – shells, driftwood, anything that interests her. And she likes gardening. I could see a likeness to her as well. It's all in the genes.

We saw several of our nieces' homes, and they were all very well designed. All on one level, open plan, light and airy.

We were now nearly at the end of our time in Australia. What wonderful memories we have of our trips to this country that we will have for the rest of our lives. We had been made so welcome by everyone, and I am so proud to be part of their family.

Chapter 8
The full Monty

I HAVE written this book as a record for the generations to follow, so that they will know how this all happened and the story of the events that led up to the sudden appearance of a new set of aunts, great aunts, uncles and great uncles — and of course sisters!

This journey in so many ways has been life-changing, and it continues to be a wonderful adventure.

During my research I soon began to realise that we have an amazing family history! There is a programme on one of our TV channels called *Who Do You Think You Are?* This is about celebrities' family histories. I often think our family history is much more interesting! I think the producers would have some very interesting stories if they researched ordinary people's family histories. There is a rich source of material just waiting to be discovered.

My own research continues, and I am planning to go to Amsterdam to discover more about our Dutch connections. We know that our Dutch grandfather, Jachabus De Latte, came to England in 1908. He worked as a hotel waiter in various hotels throughout the country. In 1915 he applied for nationalisation to be a British citizen. I have his papers and they are full of information. There is an account of the hotels he worked in, and some appear to be quite up market.

While he was working as a waiter he also tried to be accepted by the British Army as an interpreter, as he spoke four languages — Dutch, English, French and German.

However, the army decided it had enough interpreters already who were British-born, and therefore didn't need to use naturalised subjects.

He then successfully applied to join the Grenadier Guards. Unfortunately, his army records were all destroyed, among many others during a Second World War blitz, but I do know from our sister Julia that he took part in the Battle of the Somme in 1916 and was gassed.

He married Ethel Gertrude Newman in 1910 in Dalston, Hackney, London. The marriage certificate states that Jachabus's father, our great-grandfather, was a master watchmaker, and Ethel's father was an engine driver. Ethel was a hotel clerk at The London and North Western Hotel in Liverpool, so maybe that's where they met. In 1912 our mother, Ethel Wilhemina, was born in Hackney.

Our father, James Hamilton Jones, was born in Edgbaston Birmingham in 1894. His father was William Henry Jones, and his mother was Katherine Grace Helener Farrar. They had six children: Katherine May (who became a suffragette), William, Sydney, James (our father), Norman and Edward, who sadly died in infancy. Our great-grandmother Katherine had a sister called Maud, who was Field Marshall Montgomery's mother! So Monty was our great uncle!

To speed up my research, I decided to use a family research company in Canterbury, Kent, called Achievements. They were a great help, and with their expertise they were able to unearth some interesting facts.

One of the first things they did for me was to find out more about our three great uncles, whom I knew had been killed in the First World War. But I had no details of the circumstances. I was so pleased when they were able to find out quite a bit about them. Their names were Frank, Collins and Charles, and they were born in Worcester. Charles and Collins served with the Royal Warwickshire regiment, as lance corporals, and were both killed within a day of each other in the Somme in July 1916. Frank served with the Royal Horse Artillery and the Royal Field Artillery as a gunner and was killed in March 1917.

So their poor parents lost two sons within a day of each other, and the third son just eight months later. Dreadful. The researchers tried to find their service records, but sadly they were all destroyed during the Second World War. Recently, however, a friend of mine has been able to find where Frank and Collins are buried. Frank is in the Duisans British Cemetery, at Etrun, in France and Collins is buried at Delville Wood Cemetery, Longueval. Charles is remembered on the Somme memorial at Thiepval. I am so grateful to Susan for finding out this information for me.

I decided that I would like to see the places where my great uncles had fought and were buried and remembered. So in May 2016, one hundred years after the Battle of the Somme, Cliff and I joined a trip organised by a company called Historical Trips, who specialise in visiting battle fields of the First and Second World Wars.

It was all very well organised, we stayed in an old monastery in Arras, with a group that consisted of about twenty five people of all ages. They were a very interesting group of people and we enjoyed talking to them, particularly over dinner in the evening.

One of our guides was Sir Max Hastings, a renowned historian, who has written many books on the First and Second World Wars. Our other guide was Professor Gary Sheffield, who was also a very well-known First World War academic.

On our first day, we were taken by coach to Delville Wood, where the two brothers Collins and Charles fought and were killed; they were in the Royal Warwickshire Regiment. Professor Gary Sheffield explained how this battle was won and lost several times and was a turning point in the Battle of the Somme. Collins is buried at the cemetery there, but unfortunately there was not time to find his grave; I will go back at a later date to find it. But at least now I know where he fought and where he is buried. Charles is remembered at the Somme Memorial at Thiepval.

On the same day that I was taken to the memorial, and as I had the details of where Charles' name was inscribed, I tried to find him. I found the correct pillar and looked up, just at my eye level there he was, Charles Victor James. I felt quite emotional and I am so happy to have found the brothers. Frank, the third brother, was killed the following year in 1917 and is buried at Duisans British Cemetery at Etrun in France; I will make a journey at another time to find him.

I have mentioned before that Field Marshal Bernard Montgomery was our great uncle. He was born in Kennington, London during November 1887. His maternal grandfather was Frederic William Farrar, a very remarkable Victorian gentleman, and our great-great uncle. He was originally a school teacher and became a prolific author. He published some 75 books! His most famous novel was called *Eric, or, Little by Little*, written in 1858, when he was 27. It was translated into many languages, and ran to over 50 editions. It is about English school life in the 19th century, similar to Tom Brown's Schooldays, a moralistic book written by Thomas Hughes a year earlier, in 1857. Our great grandfather's book was partly autobiographical, highly moralistic in tone, and it made a strong impression on Monty in his early life.

Frederic Farrar had a very forceful personality and total faith in his own judgement, and was able to make quick and accurate decisions to a remarkable degree. These qualities were passed on in full to his grandson.

Farrar took holy orders and was made an honorary chaplain to Queen Victoria, an unusual honour for a school teacher. She liked him for his rebelliousness against the existing education system. In 1871 he was made headmaster of prestigious Marlborough College. Four years later, Prime Minister Benjamin Disraeli appointed him as rector of the influential and important St Margaret's Church, in the grounds of Westminster Abbey. His powerful sermons were so popular that the congregation had to reserve seats, often sitting on the steps of the pulpit itself! After his death, a nearby street was named after him.

While at St Margaret's, Farrar appointed a former pupil from Harrow as his curate, the Rev Henry Montgomery, the son of an Indian civil servant, Sir Robert Montgomery, who during the Siege of Lucknow in 1858 had earned the reputation of being as brave as a lion and as gentle as a lamb, and went on to become Lieutenant-Governor of the Punjab.

Shortly after arriving at St. Margaret's, the Rev Henry became engaged to the Dean's daughter, Maud, then aged just 14! They were married two years later. Before she was 25, she'd had five of her nine children! Bernard was number four. His father Henry was very influenced by his father-in-law's sermons from the pulpit on the evils of the demon drink, based on his experiences in the East End of London. Eventually, Henry took the pledge, passing on his obsession against the demon drink down through two generations of the Montgomery family.

He was never able to match his father-in-law in his achievements, as far as Maud was concerned, who referred to him as a plodder! She remarked on his most distinguished achievement being his ability to jump in one bound up the steps of Trinity College, Oxford (an almost impossible feat!).

However, in 1889, Henry was appointed Bishop of Tasmania. Bernard was two years old, and they were there until 1901.

Frederic was appointed as Canon of Westminster 1876, Archdeacon of Westminster 1883, Chaplain to the House of Commons 1890 - 95, Deputy Clerk of the Closet to Queen

Victoria, Chaplain-in-Ordinary and Deputy Clerk of the Closet to King Edward VII 1901, and Dean of Canterbury 1895-1903.

He died at the Deanery, Canterbury, in 1903, and is buried in the Cloisters. There is a memorial plaque to him near the main entrance to Canterbury Cathedral, and also two windows elsewhere to his memory.

Chapter 9
Lesley's story

I THOUGHT it would be interesting to ask Lesley and Julia if they could put into words what it was like for them and their family to find their sisters. First up, this is Lesley's account:

Late September 2010:
I had just got home from work when my husband Mark told me there was a letter for me. Thinking this must be from the doctor's surgery, inviting me to come along to do a test given to middle-aged ladies, I took the letter upstairs, opening it before I started to change from work clothes to more comfortable ones.

My interest started to build when reading the opening paragraph. It read; "I hope you will be able to help with an inquiry I have received. I do not know if you are aware that the adoption law changed in December 2005, and birth relatives can now ask for an approach to be made to their relatives who were adopted. AAA-Norcap is a registered intermediary agency undertaking this work. Sarah Young would welcome news of her sister, who was born in 1955."

At this point, I think I said "NO" out loud! This is what I had waited for for the last 55 years! My heart was racing and I felt in a total state of shock.

I took the letter downstairs to Mark, who was watching television, and said to him: "I think you'd better look at this." He took the letter from me, he was half looking at the screen and half reading the letter, then he turned the TV off, read the letter again and said: "Well, Lesley, this is the kind of letter that could change your life." And it certainly has done!

From a very young age my adoptive parents, especially my mother, told me the story of my birth and early life. That is definitely the best course of action, and I can thank them for that. I was made aware that I had two other sisters, the eldest being 21 years older than me, but her name was never spoken of, and the younger being three years older, and her name was Sarah.

From around the age of ten I would often think about my sisters and, thinking back, I felt I was in a situation where I did not belong. At around this time my adoptive mother took me to visit the children's home where Sarah and I were placed as small children. She was friendly with the matron there. As they chatted, the subject of my eldest sister was raised, my mother was told that she had married and emigrated to Australia.

On hearing this news my heart sank – as far as I was concerned Australia may as well have been the moon, and it seemed so far away there was probably no way I would ever meet her. But somehow, I don't know why, I kept the thought that Sarah would one day find me.

The next day I phoned Linda Cherry, the intermediary for Norcap. She was thrilled to hear from me, and asked what I knew about my adoption. I explained that my adoptive parents had always been very open and honest about details surrounding the situation. She asked if I knew I had siblings. I said I had two other sisters, one being 21 years older than me, the other three years older.

Then came the next shock! I was told: "You are actually one of four girls!" Another sister had been adopted out of the family, ten years earlier. Her name at the time was Penelope, and she was the sister who had made the approach, and since the adoption had been renamed Sarah.

Linda then asked what my husband's thoughts were about this news. I told her we had discussed this and he was fine with the idea of making contact, but was concerned that I would not be hurt. Linda said it wouldn't be a problem, that she had been working with Sarah for some time, and that she was a lovely lady. She asked if I would like a letter that Sarah had written and some photos of her. "Yes please!" I replied.

Within the next two days I received the handwritten letter, plus photos of Sarah with her two dogs. Seeing these pictures, my first reaction was: that's me! Wearing jeans and a fleece, taking the dogs for a walk. And it felt right.

Before I phoned Linda back, we decided we would tell our two daughters of these developments and gauge their reaction. Mark phoned our youngest, Cheryl, who was very excited about the news and wanted to know when she could meet Sarah. My husband cautioned her in saying we were a long way from that.

He then phoned our eldest, Gemma, who was surprised but very cautious saying: "You need to be very careful – you don't know what you are getting into."

I was cautious at first and considered that perhaps a letter would be best, at this time. Then I had a rethink. I phoned Linda and agreed she could pass on my phone number to Sarah. Within fifteen minutes the phone rang. My husband answered and said: "Hello, Sarah, I guess you'd like to speak to Lesley."

Her first words to me were: "I can't believe I'm speaking to my sister!"

We seemed to flow into a conversation, without a trace of awkwardness. During the conversation, Sarah told me she had made contact with our eldest sister Julia in Australia by phone. Julia had been thrilled when she received the letter from Norcap and was eager to speak to Sarah. During their conversation Julia said to Sarah: "Of course there is another one of us you know!" And she told her of the baby who had been born to our mother during the mid-1950s. The situation at the time must have been very difficult for our mother. She had lost her husband six months before I was born, and with that and having a three-year-old to care for, the whole situation got too much for her, and it sounds as if she was suffering from depression. As a result, things came to a head and Sarah and I were placed into care, at a children's home in Winchester. She did not feel she could cope with a baby, so it was decided that I would be put up for adoption. But as far as Sarah was concerned, our mother was going to try to look after her, as soon as she felt well enough.

So as a result of this conversation with Julia, Sarah found out about me, and started to search for me, something I will always be eternally grateful for. As a result of her search I found out about her. If the contact with Julia had never happened, Sarah would never have known about me.

Once adopted, each individual is given a new identity and just disappears into a new life. It is a strange phenomenon, but I always thought, quite early in life, that Sarah would one day come and find me — but the thing is it didn't turn out to be the Sarah I thought it would be.

Soon after that initial phone call, Sarah sent some photos she had been sent by Julia of our real mother and father. She told me she would be doing this, and I couldn't wait. At long last I was going to see a picture of my mother, something I had dreamt of for so long. I knew I would never meet her, as she was 45 when I was born, and so many years had since passed that she would surely be no longer alive.

Once again I returned from work to find a brown envelope on the doormat — this was it! This was what I had been waiting for all these years, to see a photo of my mother. In the envelope was a picture of Julia in her twenties, with our grandparents, our mother's parents, and a more up-to-date picture of Julia in her garden. Another photo was of our father, then when I saw our mother, something quite out of character happened: I burst into tears.

I felt as though I was in a dream, something I never thought would happen had come true. The picture showed her sitting with a friend on a beach. I knew which one she was instantly. It was like looking in a mirror. Yes, I do look like her, something I had always wondered about.

In the weeks following that initial phone call, Sarah and I talked on the phone several times, and we were both eager to meet up, so a date was arranged, and the venue was to be Windsor Castle.

October 10, 2010

The tenth day of the tenth month was a special day in more ways than one. This was the day I would meet my sister. It was a Sunday, and to say I was nervous is an understatement. We arranged to meet up at midday. We travelled down from our home in the Cotswolds, and the nearer we got, the quieter I got. Mark and I had discussed what Sarah and Cliff would be like — would they be a couple we liked?

Mark said: "Well, we will either get on well, or they will be the kind of people we will send a Christmas card to once a year."

We arrived in good time and parked up near the castle. We walked up the hill to the castle when Mark's mobile rang. It was Cliff, Sarah's husband, telling us they had initially lost their way to Windsor from Kent, but they were now looking for a parking space. Mark told him we would be waiting at an entrance to the hotel opposite the castle.

So there we were, waiting and watching a sea of people coming up the hill, thinking 'Is that them, could that couple be them?' At this time in October, Windsor was far more packed with tourists than we had imagined. Then, quite out of character, Mark told me to stay put, and he was going to look for them. Normally he would be the one to hide behind me in this sort of situation.

After a few minutes, he walked towards this couple coming up the hill and said: "You must be Cliff, and you must be Sarah. I'm Mark, and Lesley is over there in front of the hotel."

Sarah asked: "How did you know?"

Mark replied: "Looking into your eyes is like looking into my wife's eyes."

As they approached the hotel a rush of excitement came over me. Sarah and I gave each other a big hug, and I remember thinking 'Gosh, she does look like me!' Then Cliff introduced himself, and I gave him a big hug.

After talking over our journey and parking problems, Cliff invited us to have a coffee (something we now know he likes) at the hotel.

Sarah had a huge folder with her containing all the information, records of births, marriages and death certificates, a result of her research she had gathered over the ten years this research has taken, while I only had a letter given to me by my adoptive parents, giving details of my mother, father and known siblings, and correspondence that was passed to them prior to my formal adoption.

As we sat drinking coffee and getting to know each another, I looked through this folder with utter amazement at the amount of work that had gone into the research. We chatted about the journey that had led us to this day, and the families we had, after meeting our partners.

After a while it was decided we should all go and look for somewhere to have lunch. Sarah and I strolled along the pavement, arm in arm, chatting about our lives, followed by Mark and Cliff, chatting to each another.

It seemed unreal that after all these years apart we should have the opportunity to do this.

Over lunch, Sarah told us about the phone conversations she had had with our sister Julia in Australia, and what a lot they had in common, especially anything to do with gardening. She asked me if I had been in touch with her, which had not happened at that point in time. To me it was a case of one step at a time, something I had to get my head around, plus the fact that the very sister I thought had been lost forever had been found.

While walking back to our cars, Sarah talked about Julia and Australia and said: "We are going." Thinking they had already booked the trip, Mark and I were somewhat surprised, then she said: "Come with us!"

Well, that was another bolt out of the blue! Australia was a place I would not consider going to in a million years, much too far for me, not being a confident flyer.

We all said our goodbyes, and went home with a lot to think about, but we both reflected on what a success the day had been, and that Cliff and Sarah were certainly worth more than a Christmas card once a year. In fact, over time we have become very good friends, and regularly meet up.

As time went on, thoughts about going to Australia started to make me think, 'Why not?' Something started to drive me into thinking this. It must have been the thought of meeting my other sister, Julia.

Eventually, I plucked up the courage to phone Julia. I have never phoned abroad before, never mind the other side of the world and speaking to a stranger. I also worried about the time difference, not wanting to ring in the middle of the night.

I phoned the number with a special code in front, which gave us a call rate of a 1p a minute. After a while Julia answered. I told her it was Lesley, her sister, calling from the UK. She seemed pleased to hear me and we just talked about what had happened with the family search, and how surprised she was at all that had happened.

She told me she had six children, and the circumstances that led her and her husband Michael to emigrate in 1958 as '£10 Poms'.

I told her a bit about my family, and we touched on bits of information about our parents. Before I knew it, an hour had flown and it was time to draw the conversation to a close, before it started costing God knows what!

Afterwards, when I put the phone down, it was way past my bedtime, but my mind was racing. I couldn't believe what an easy conversation it had been, given the fact that although related, we were in fact strangers. I reflected that she had a kind, gentle Australian accent, and it felt as though we had known each other for years.

Soon the four of us started to think about a trip of a lifetime to Australia, to see Julia and her family. We also wanted to take the opportunity to see this vast continent. None of us knew really where to begin, but Mark decided to get in touch with a company that specialises in tailor-made trips around Australia. After several conversations with Christine, who was so helpful, an itinerary over a month was planned, which also included a two-night stopover in Singapore to break the journey, as to us it seemed such a long way to go without a break. The plan allowed us to visit Sydney, then on for a three-day stay in Nowra to meet Julia and her family. We also factored in a trip on the Indian Pacific train from Sydney to Melbourne, then an internal flight to Cairns to see the Great Barrier Reef. Then finally the flight home via Hong Kong for three days.

When Mark ran this past me I remember thinking, 'Oh no! Not another plane journey!' But I was prepared to go along with this as it was a chance to see as much as we could in the month we had.

Mark put the plan to Sarah and Cliff, and they thought it sounded great. The next problem was the cost and how we could possibly afford it. Mark got to work on several ideas of how to raise some cash. For some time he had wondered whether we were in the wrong council tax band, and we had overpaid. He researched several properties in our street, and discovered they were on a lower rating. He wrote to the council, giving details of what he had found. Some time passed and then we received a letter, saying the matter had been looked into, and the findings were in our favour. We had been on the wrong band and were due for a refund – and even better news that we would be refunded for every year we had lived there, this being 15 years! It amounted to a large sum of money: more than enough to pay for the trip.

On top of this, we had a call from a firm who looked into insurance mis-selling and could help recover an overpayment. We decided to look into this, and sure enough we had a case, which was looked into and once again we were awarded a payout – more towards the holiday fund!

That same year in December the mail arrived one morning with a card from Mark's uncle. When I opened it, to my shock and surprise, out fell a cheque for £1,000, with a short note suggesting we put this money towards the trip to Australia, with his good wishes.

When Mark came home from work he was as shocked as me at this news. This kind of good fortune just never happens to us. So with one thing and another, almost the whole trip was covered by the most unexpected means, almost as though it was meant to be!

During the coming months waiting for the day we were to fly to Singapore, for the start of our adventure, I began to think, 'What the hell am I doing? This trip is throwing me so far out of my comfort zone, it is unbelievable'. It was to be quite a full-on trip, with all the flights and travelling, but something was driving me on, I can't explain what.

The big day arrived, and our eldest daughter Gemma and her husband took time off work to drive us to Heathrow. They picked us up at 3pm. I was so nervous, I could hardly eat the brunch I had cooked that morning. We arrived at Terminal 4 and said our hasty goodbyes to Tom and Gemma, as they needed to get back rather than try parking. The terminal doors opened, we waved goodbye, and went and located Sarah and Cliff, and started the second phase of this most remarkable journey.

October 30th, 2011.

The day eventually arrived when we would meet Julia for the first time. We had spent the last few days in Sydney, phoned Julia on the second day to confirm we would be arriving on the Sunday and at what time the train was due. After an early breakfast we headed to the train station in Sydney. Mark was on a mission that day. He knew what time our train was due to depart for Nowra, as we had all been to the station the previous day to check how far it was from our apartment in Pitt Street, and to check on train times.

Mark was charging ahead and we all followed as best we could (I don't think Cliff will ever forget that morning), with our cases and bags in tow. We arrived at the station exhausted, only to find the train we wanted had been cancelled! As luck would have it, there was an earlier one about to leave in ten minutes. So again we struggled with our luggage down a lift and on to the platform, just as the train pulled in.

The journey to Kiama took about 90 minutes, then we had to change trains for Nowra. When we arrived at Nowra, it wasn't long before Julia arrived. As soon as she appeared I knew instantly this was my sister, from the photo I had been sent. She was the spitting image of our father: tall, with very similar features. Of the three of us, Sarah and I are more like our mother. We all had a hug, and chatted about our journey, so relieved that we had arrived on time and hadn't made Julia wait on the platform for us.

We piled into Julia's car, just as well she had an estate car, as it took all of us plus our luggage with ease. On the way to Julia's house she mentioned she needed to stop at the local shopping mall for bread.

"That's fine," said Cliff. "It will give us a chance to have a coffee!"

As we sat talking I noticed Julia was looking at me so intently. Then I got up to go to the ladies. When I returned, Mark said: "Julia was just telling us how much you resemble your mother." It was almost uncanny.

We carried on chatting and finished our coffee, visited the supermarket, then headed to Julia's home, where she and husband Michael had cultivated a strawberry farm. Sadly, Michael passed away some years ago and Julia now lives on her own.

We arrived at lunchtime, had some sandwiches, while Julia looked out as many photos as she could find, explaining that many were lost in a flood. But what we saw were very interesting. We saw some of our mother and father, plus one or two of my sister Sarah, who is three years older then me. It turned out that she had actually ended up going to Australia, when she was about twelve. She lived with Julia for a while and then stayed with other family members.

Later that day, a barbecue had been planned, to give us the opportunity to meet Julia's daughters. One by one they arrived with their partners and children. It became quite overwhelming and I couldn't begin to remember all the names. It seemed unreal that I had this second family on the other side of the world. They all thought it was amazing that three sisters could be reunited after all this time. There was much to talk about and photos to take, plus kangaroo steaks on the barbie, washed down with good Aussie beer!

The next day the family had planned a boat trip to see the whales in Jervis Bay. Julia picked us up from the guest house, and took us to her favourite coffee shop, where one or two of her daughters joined us. Julia would come out with snippets of information about our parents, much of which she had chosen to forget. Julia had told us that she liked to watch British comedy on TV. I asked her if she'd ever watched

Absolutely Fabulous. Immediately she answered, saying: "There's a character in that who is a dead ringer for our mother." I replied that she was starting to sound like Eddy played by Jennifer Saunders in the comedy! We all laughed.

At that moment it became clear as to why our mother was unable to care for us all, if that was what her personality was like. It gave me a greater understanding of the whole story, and answered the big question: Why? How could she not only give me away, but my sister as well?

The whale-watching trip was amazing – what a unique experience. Afterwards we returned to Julia's home, where she cooked dinner for us then dropped us back at the guest house. This was to be our last day in Nowra and we probably wouldn't see Julia again, as she did not like goodbyes. However, her daughter had mentioned that they would possibly meet up with us again, for a day in Sydney.

We then went on the Indian Pacific train to Adelaide and then Melbourne, before returning to Sydney. We spent three days in Sydney, and we heard nothing from them. Then on the evening before the last day, we had a call from Katherine to let us know she and Julia were planning to get the train the next day to spend the day with us.

On the last day we all met up, along with Katherine's daughters. We had a wonderful day together, talking and shopping, and ended it with a fabulous meal in a restaurant overlooking Sydney Opera House. As we walked back to the street where we were to say our final goodbyes, Julia said: "I think our mother would be glad that we all found one another." With tears in our eyes we had to leave them.

Julia's parting words were: "Perhaps we will come to the UK, to visit you next time!"

This I did not expect, but sure enough that is what happened the very next year! We were able to take her and Katherine back to Bournemouth and revisit old haunts that she and Michael knew when they first met.

We had all spent such a wonderful time together in Australia, and the icing on the cake was the family making us so welcome. It was a very special experience I shall never forget.

In 2013, we visited Australia again, landing in Perth and travelling by train over three days across to Sydney. We spent a few fabulous days in Sydney, and then travelled down to Nowra to spend two weeks with Julia and her family. They rented a house near the beach at Jervis Bay, and the time we spent there was absolute magic.

Chapter 10
Julia's story

I WAS born on April 16th, 1934, to James and Ethel Wilhelmina Jones. Unlike my sisters, I did live with my parents for a short time while I was young. I remember the house by the sea at Hengistbury Head, near Bournemouth. I remember my dad – being on the beach with him and sitting in the back of his car, which had lovely leather seats. I don't have a memory of my mother at that time.

When I was about five years old the war broke out and my grandparents moved to the Midlands. They decided to take me with them, perhaps to be away from the bombing – I don't know. Jack and Ethel Wilhelmina Delatte were my mother's parents, they settled in Nottingham and I was promptly sent to boarding school in the Derbyshire hills. What a difference from the lovely south coast, with its warm weather and splendid beaches.

It was not a very happy time for a little girl. My grandparents meant well but I didn't understand why I should be away from my parents. It was hard to have friends in Nottingham because the girls at school came from different towns. Our school was situated in a small village where we were kept quite separate. We only saw other children on a Sunday when we all went to church in the village, walking in two by two (like Madeline). I often thought how nice it would be to have a brother or sister and to live with my parents −but that wasn't going to happen.

One day, towards the end of the war, my grandmother read aloud a letter for my father saying that they had had a baby girl but she would be adopted out. Granny and Pop both seemed to think it was a good idea. "How sad," I thought. They named her Penelope Valentine.

Anyone brought up in the war will remember the expectations we had of what life was going to be like after the war; in my case it meant going back to Hampshire and, I thought, to my parents – but this was not so.

I stayed with Granny and Pop and was sent to another boarding school (weekly this time).

In 1953 we heard that my parents had another daughter, Sarah. She was born at home in Christchurch and it seemed that my parents were going to keep this daughter, but I learnt that there were times when Sarah was sent away to a children's home, before returning to our parents for a while. Just what my mother's problems were I didn't really know, except that she had a problem with alcohol.

My sister Zoe was born in 1955 and that same year my father died suddenly.

I left my grandparents and rushed off to help my mother, who now had two small children to look after. While living with my mother I had found work. One day I came home from work to find both of the girls had been taken to a children's home.

That same year I met Michael Morley. He had to serve his two years' National Service and I thought we would be married after that time, but Michael thought otherwise – and we were married a week before he started his National Service.

Two years later, he came home from Germany. I was soon pregnant, working in Boots the chemist's, living in a one-room flat, which we had to vacate, and Michael had no job – what to do? I had an aunt, my father's sister Katherine, who lived in Australia, and she agreed to nominate us for emigration. Three months later we were on the Fairsea, chartered by the Australian Government to transport immigrants from Britain, heading for New South Wales and the unknown.

Meanwhile, Sarah had returned to our mother but Zoe had been adopted. Michael agreed that when we got settled we would send for Sarah and she would live with us, but that didn't eventuate until she was nine years old and I was about to have my third child. We were living on a dairy farm in Kangaroo Valley, New South Wales. We had our son Roger, who was born only three months after our arrival in Australia, then Katherine two years later, followed by Sarah coming from England; then our daughter Tanya, born the same year. Sharon was born in 1964, then Kerrie in 1968, and Gillian in 1971.

I often thought of my sisters and wondered where they were. I hoped that they had a better life with their adopted parents; I didn't think that I would ever see them.

One day I had a phone call from Linda, who worked for Norcap, and she told me that she had a contact with Penelope Valentine (now Sarah Young) and asked if I'd like to be contacted by her. What a shock and thrill!

The next evening at 7pm the phone rang. I picked it up and said: "Hello Sarah." We talked for hours and I was able to tell her about Zoe and Sarah. She contacted Zoe, who is now named Lesley, in a short time and it was not long before we met up. They came to Australia with their husbands, Cliff and Mark. What a good time we had discovering our family and aunts, nieces and nephews. This all came about because of the hard work that Sarah put in after her adoptive parents had died and also because of the wonderful work of Norcap.

It is difficult to say why our mother could not look after herself; she probably suffered from depression of some sort. I am sure she would be happy to know that her four girls have met up and will have many years ahead with close contact.

Thank you, Norcap.

And so this remarkable journey continues…

THE END

My birth family tree

Our parents:

James Hamilton Jones, born April 14th, 1894, in Birmingham, and Ethel Wilhelmina Delatte, born May 4th, 1911, at 188 Kennington Road, Lambeth, London.

Four daughters:

- Julia Morley – born April 6th, 1934, at Bournemouth. Now living in Nowra, New South Wales, Australia.
- Sarah Young – born Penelope Valentine, February 14th, 1945, in Southbourne, Bournemouth. Adopted in October 1945. Now living in Faversham, Kent.
- Sarah Hamilton Jones – born April 4th, 1953, in Christchurch, Dorset. Now living in New Zealand.
- Lesley Pratley – born Zoe Elizabeth, July, 24th, 1955, at Barton-on-sea, near Bournemouth. Adopted in January 1957, now living in Cirencester, Gloucestershire.

Acknowledgements

This remarkable story could never have happened without the help given to me by so many lovely people.

First and foremost is our Norcap intermediary, Linda Cherry. Without her expertise and support, we sisters would never have been reunited. We are all so grateful to her. Words cannot really express how much we appreciate all her hard work.

It is with great sadness that I have to report that unfortunately Norcap has had to close down because of financial problems. Luckily, however, Linda has been able to continue to do her invaluable work as a freelance intermediary. It is good to know that she is able to help people in situations like us.

There have been several times in this journey of discovery that the right person has just turned up at the right time, with skills to help me. One of these people was Nancy, an old school friend of my daughter-in-law Bea. Nancy has a keen interest in family history. When she learnt about my story, she was very keen to help find out about some of our relatives. She found our great grandparents, and our great-great grandparents! And she put me in touch with Bournemouth Library, and their amazing family records department, who discovered I had sisters! So thank you, Nancy from all of us, you were a big link in the chain!

We must also thank Bournemouth Library for their help. I shall never forget getting the information about my sisters.

Our thanks must also go to my friend Sue, who is also very interested and has gained a lot of knowledge on genealogy. She, like Nancy, never gives up when presented with some query or other. She is still finding things out! She recently found out where our great-great uncle, William Frederic Farrar, the Dean of Canterbury, is buried, one of only a few burials in the cathedral cloisters. She also managed to track down where our great uncles, three brothers, all killed at the Somme in the First World War, are buried. I am so pleased to know where they are. Thank you, Sue!

I must mention Gerry, who first told me about Norcap. If we hadn't had that conversation, we would not be where we are today! Thank you, Gerry and Maureen, for being such good friends.

I would also like to thank Gill and Brian (teachers!) who have helped me with editing, and a big thank-you to Jean for helping me with the technical stuff involved with the final typing up of this endeavour to record for future generations this remarkable story.

A very special thanks to Jim Bruce (www.ebooklover.co.uk), my editor. He has been so patient with me and guided me through every stage.

Finally, my grateful thanks to my dear husband Cliff. He has been so supportive to me, and I am eternally grateful to him. Thank you also to my sons, John and Robert, for listening to their mum talk endlessly about their aunties – just look at their family tree now!

Printed in Great Britain
by Amazon